EVIDENCE THAT WE ARE DESCENDED FROM CHAIRS

Poems By
Andrew Merton

Accents Publishing ▪ Lexington KY ▪ 2012

Copyright © 2012 by Andrew Merton
All rights reserved

Printed in the United States of America

Accents Publishing
Editor: Katerina Stoykova-Klemer
Cover Illustration: Frédéric Bazille, *Portrait of Pierre-Auguste Renoir*, 1867
Designer: Simeon Kondev

Library of Congress Control Number: 2011963553
ISBN: 978-1-936628-09-4
First Edition
10 9 8 7 6 5 4 3 2 1

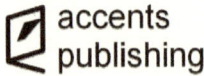

Accents Publishing is an independent press for brilliant voices. For a catalog of current and upcoming titles, please visit us on the Web at

www.accents-publishing.com

For Gail, Gabe and Rachel

My thanks to Charles Simic and Mekeel McBride for encouraging a newspaper guy to try writing poetry back in the last millennium and for their generous guidance since then; to Shelley Girdner, Kimberly Green and Jody Hetherington for their meticulous yet kind critiques over the years; to David Rivard for his insightful suggestions on what to keep and what to cut; to L.T., without whom many of these poems would not have been written, and Alfred, without whom they would not have seen the light of day; and to Katerina, for believing.

Contents

A Pig Slits My Throat: Foreword by Charles Simic / xi

I

The Original Sin: Adam's Story / 1
Dice / 2
Evidence that We Are Descended from Chairs / 3
Preemie / 4
Smoke / 5
May 12, 1944 / 6
White Baby / 7
Intuition / 8
Bipolar / 9
A Young Mother / 10
Soap / 11
Home Movie Projector / 12
Shrimp / 13
All Hallows Eve / 14
Learning a Language / 15
Mud / 16
In the Year of the Platypus / 17
Why I Left the Poetry Reading Early / 18

II

Fire / 21
Heisenberg's Uncertainty Principle / 22
Subjunctive / 23
The Musician's Daughter / 24
First Honeymoon / 25
Cruise Ship Intervention / 26
My Mother / 27
Tequila / 28
The Poet Who Killed the Moon Pleads Guilty … / 29

III

Questions and Answers About Mustaches / 33
Valentine / 34
Twenty-two Years After Falling in Love with You / 35
Just Before Falling Asleep on a Bench near Wittgenstein's Grave / 36
Reluctant Return from England / 37
Journey to the Subconscious, Interrupted / 38
Degrees of Nudity / 39
Bricks / 40
Rachel at Eight / 41
Time Travel in the Grand Canyon / 42
First Day of Swimming Therapy for a Boy Recovering … / 43
Snow / 45
My Next Poem / 46

IV

Keys / 49
A Message from Ugarte / 50
Appalachian Nocturne / 51
The Request / 52
Counter / 53
coming out of a depression / 54
Chickens / 55
The Passion of the Eiffel Tower / 56
How I Failed to Write This Poem / 58

V

Diner, Revere, Massachusetts, Winter, 4 a.m. / 61
The Way Women Are / 62
Bodyguard / 63
One of the Starving Children in Europe Absolves Me / 64
Advice My Daughter Will Probably Ignore / 65
At 65 / 66
Immortality in a Minor Key / 67

Finding the Potato / 68

VI

Late Harvest / 71
Floater / 72
Last Peach / 73
A Widow at 93 / 74
The Death of a Scholar / 75
Advice to a Weary Traveler / 76
Alchemy / 77
Your Date with Death / 78
Judgment Day / 79

Acknowledgments / 81

About the Author / 83

A Pig Slits My Throat

At the heart of the impulse to sit down and write a poem is the astonishment that the world exists and that we are in it. How strange, I'm looking out of this window, seeing this tree and this street I so rarely notice, one says to oneself one day. How strange I had a mother and a father who told me about God and about many other things, some of which I still believe, and some of which I now make fun of. And how peculiar my own life turned out to be with all the people I have known and all the important and unimportant things I lived through, a good many of which I still can't get out of my mind. And perhaps the oddest thing of all is that I'm attempting to convey all that in a few words of a poem while suspecting that a thousand pages of writing would not do it justice.

In Andrew Merton's view of poetry, brevity is the soul of wisdom. His poems are compact. He likes plenty of white space around some image or pithy utterance. "A chair looks like a person sitting in a chair," is the entire first section of a poem called "Evidence that We Are Descended from Chairs." How true, one says to oneself. Merton is like an elderly neighbor, someone we pass on the street for years without a second look, someone who—when we finally happen to exchange a few sentences—seems to have been thinking and worrying about many of the same things we have, someone we would like to spend more time with from now on.

> God saw that I was lonely.
> He was right about that.
> The rib thing, though—
>
> consider the stars,
>
> the firmament,
> the beasts, fish,
> birds, all that.
>
> Don't tell me He had nothing left.

Almost every one of his poems has a surprise waiting for the reader, either some astonishing figure of speech or a witty observation we are not likely to forget anytime soon. "Stutterer with metal teeth/chewing up film,/spitting images" is how he describes an ancient movie projector. While the narrator in a poem entitled "Snow" sits in a booth of an empty diner, "outside, a small maple waves its branches wildly, like a cop shielding children from the sight of a corpse." In another, whose subject is seeing the world anew after coming out of depression, he notes "morels at the foot of a dead apple tree/shadow of a hawk, receding/whisper of snakes on stone/the sun that powers the heart of a flea." In the one called "My Next Poem," after promising a new poem that will shimmer across the sky like northern lights and swallow black holes, he confesses that *this* poem will in fact concern smaller things: "Milk turning sour,/the spider in the bathtub/the click at the other end of the line/the hairline crack/in the ceiling over the bed".

Merton has an elegy for his father and several poems about his late mother, but his chief subject may be described as our human comedy mixed with tragedy, everything from people falling in love, to searching for God. Even when he recounts his childhood, as in a wonderful poem "White Baby," about his black nanny Ophelia, or in a poem that describes locking himself out of his car, he has a nice humorous touch. As the Polish poet Adam Zagajewski once shrewdly observed: "Poetry is joy hiding despair. But under the despair—more joy."

Keys

At 2 a.m.
in a strange part of town

I lock myself out of my car.
Through the window I can see

my keys in the ignition,
my mobile phone on the seat,

and on the floor,
a note from a woman:

What has happened?
I feel a terrible distance between us.

There are many vastly subtle and marvelously entertaining poems in this book. Merton is wise about the ways we live. He keeps his ears and eyes open wherever he goes. He can be both tough and compassionate, describing, for example, in a poem called "Bodyguard," a big, broad-shouldered man swaggering down the street in London with his tiny and lame wife, who limps behind him, swatting at pickpockets with her crutch, and, in another poem, his dead grandmother on a park bench, feeding stale breadcrumbs to children. I believe it was the novelist Barry Hannah who said that all good writing has an element of pity in it. This is certainly true of Merton. In a poem called "Judgment Day" a pig slits his throat, a lobster drops him in boiling water and an ant the size of a building steps on him. In other words, he knows what it's like to be at the other end of the stick. And what's more, he writes beautiful poems.

Charles Simic

I

The Original Sin: Adam's Story

God saw that I was lonely.
He was right about that.
The rib thing, though—

consider the stars,

the firmament,
the beasts, fish,
birds, all that.

Don't tell me he had nothing left.

What I saw
when I saw Eve—
her long hair, breasts,
the absence between her thighs
notwithstanding—
was me.

That was all right
until the business with the snake,
the rising of my desire.

Dice

God does not play dice.
 —Einstein

Not, at least,
since that day in the garden
when He rolled snake-eyes.

Evidence that We Are Descended from Chairs

1.

A chair looks like a person sitting in a chair.

2.

A mother and child are two generations.
A mother and child in a rocking chair
are three.

3.

Astaire rarely danced with a table.

4.

Pity the candidate who debates his opponent's empty chair.

5.

Even now,
power rests
in the one we call the chair.

Preemie

The light came too soon,
hurt my eyes.
Drew me, screaming,
down a tunnel
into New York City
where I slept late,
wore dark glasses,
rode the subways,
lived in a woman's
sunless apartment.
Then one day
I buried my mother.
Caught a glimpse
of another tunnel.
Now I wake at dawn.

Smoke

On July 31, 1932, the Nazis won 229 seats in the Reichstag,
while in Frankfurt, the Jew who would become my father
sank a sixteen-foot putt
to become, for a month or so,

the top-ranking golfer in Germany.
He was nineteen. His prize, a silver cigarette box,
was one of the few things he brought with him
six years later, on the boat to New York.

He was a short, strong man, built to withstand wind.
He wore a trench coat and a fedora.
Often a cigarette hung from his lips.
Whether any of this attracted the Jew who would become my mother

I cannot say. Maybe it was just that they were in the same boat,
steaming away from the cauldron. As for the rest:
After Europe burned he built a business.
Fathered two children.

Bought a ranch house on Long Island.
Was cremated after dying young,
on the fourteenth green of a country club in Queens,
his putter in one hand, a smoke in the other.

May 12, 1944

I arrived a week early
with eleven toes

but the Allies broke through in Italy,
women got the vote in Bermuda,

and a man in Louisville, Kentucky,
was granted a patent

for waterproof cigarette paper
treated with aluminum,

so none of the newspapers
took note of my birth.

As for my family,
my brother was at school,

my father at war.
My mother was in a scopolamine trance.

There was no one to greet me
but the black cocker spaniel

who later taught me to crawl.

White Baby

(Greenwich Village, New York, 1948)

I am four and small and white. My nanny, Ophelia,
is brown and solid as the women's penitentiary on Eighth Avenue.
The penitentiary doesn't say much, but in the end it will say
    enough.

Ophelia speaks to me as though I were a grownup. Andy, she says,
I want you to meet my brother William and my sister Belle.
Belle and William, shake hands with Andy.

It does not matter that Belle and William are invisible.
The four of us talk about William's job cleaning toilets at the
    racetrack
and Belle's rotten boyfriend, Ivan. We even talk about my mother,

who wants me to call her by her first name. Your momma's a fine
    woman,
says Ophelia, but you got no more business calling her Felice
than I do. You just keep on calling her Momma, and she'll come to
    her senses.

William and Belle agree. Sure enough,
Momma comes to her senses, and after that
things are fine until one day she joins us for a walk.

As we pass the penitentiary a woman calls from above:
Hey Ophelia! Where'd you get that white baby?
I don't see any baby. After that I don't see Ophelia

or William or Belle anymore either.
My new nanny, Lily, is so pale she makes me look brown.
Lily hardly speaks at all.

Intuition

(featuring the late Burt Lancaster in a supporting role)

The six of them squeeze into a booth in a seedy diner just outside Newark:

a balding child dressed as a monk

a woman with eels for fingers

an ambulance driver munching a ladder

an alligator wrapped in a boa

the late Burt Lancaster

and a swarthy, mustachioed man
with ammunition belts crisscrossing his chest,
who gazes fearfully at his companions
before revealing himself
as the great-grandson of Pancho Villa
and muttering through clenched teeth:
One of you spent time as a violist.
I can just feel it.

Bipolar

The crows are elsewhere today.

Shovel the coal from your eyelids.

Empty the wheelbarrow of your mind.

Regurgitate a circus.

Indulge your clamoring toes.

Shake out your sheets until all the potatoes are gone.

Make love to an iris, a pansy, a rose.

Discover the constellation Platypus.

Hurry. The crows are never gone for long.

A Young Mother
(1950)

To escape the tangle
she becomes her sewing needle

plunging through the fabric
of her sea blue blouse.

Again and again
she dives and surfaces,

a skipping stone,
a cormorant,

a marlin
at play in the frozen mists

of the North Atlantic.
Such is her joy

that for minutes, months,
whole seasons at a time,

she is able to forget
the line through her tale.

Soap

A teacher said we would make soap out of lye.
Be careful, it can burn you,
it can blind you.

They had lied to my uncle,
blinded him, burned him,
made soap of him.

I fled the classroom with dirty hands.

Home Movie Projector
(1955)

Stutterer with metal teeth
chewing up film,
spitting images.

Shrimp

Your mother calls you *sea monkey*,
confirming what you have long suspected:

she sent for you with a coupon
from the back of a Batman comic book.

When you arrived
she put you in a bowl of water

where, according to the guarantee,
you were supposed to do tricks.

But what do you know of tricks?
It is all you can do to keep moving,

to avoid looking up
at that shimmering face,

that enormous mouth.

All Hallows Eve

I taste my mother's ashes
and creep into the night.
There I find

Hansel, alone.

Charred St. Joan
tapping on someone's door.

The little Dutch boy's withered finger.

And my dead grandmother
on a park bench
feeding stale breadcrumbs
to children.

Learning a Language

One summer my father gave me a ticket
to Peru. Said it was time I learned a language.
Said to be careful of the girls there.
He needn't have worried; I didn't know enough

not to. "Never buy a cow
when you can get the milk for free,"
he explained, and winked.
I said sure. I didn't like milk anyway.

He sent me to a town on the Amazon
where a friend of his sold toilets
to people who had no plumbing.
I had a room, a jeep, a rifle,

and *Vanity Fair*, paperback,
two inches thick, required reading
which I avoided by going to the movies.
German, with Spanish subtitles.

I learned neither,
but met an Englishman
who said he'd teach me about girls.
He could have started anywhere.

One day he did. Caught me staring.
"You don't just stare at them," he said,
"it makes them nervous. You have to smile."
He smiled, got the girl, borrowed the jeep.

I walked home,
propped Thackeray against the wall
and fired. Wrote home: "Halfway through
Vanity Fair."

Mud

(Emerging from a round of shock therapy, 2007)

In the summer of 1961, on the edge of the Peruvian rain forest, a boy from New York borrowed old Luis Araña's jeep. Luis was as brown as cured tobacco. He swore he was pure Castilian. Luis swore by his jeep, too. It had no starter. He warned: Be sure to park it on a hill. Especially in the rain. Never linger on the flats. If you stall, we have to search for you, pull you out. Maybe the jaguars get you first.

The boy roared up inclines, plunged down slopes and shunned level ground until he stalled out. Now he mumbles through the haze: Luis, listen to me please. It's not the jaguars that get you, or even the spiders or snakes. The thing that gets you is the god-damned mud.

In the Year of the Platypus

each letter will be written
to whom it may not concern.

Tomatoes will cease their laughter.

Curmudgeons will sprout
from the eyes of wayward potatoes.

Frogs will braid a tapestry of doom.

The lion shall petition to lie down
with another lion.

At long last, the martyred Moby Dick
will tell his side of the story.

Ukuleles, kazoos and accordions will inherit the earth.

As for me, you will find me
disguised as an inkstand,
trembling in anticipation
of the Year of the Squid.

Why I Left the Poetry Reading Early

I wanted to applaud
after the very first poem,
in which the famous poet

revealed the secrets of the universe
and the human soul
with no more effort than a shrug.

The second poem put the first to shame.
I was forced to restrain myself
by gripping the edges of my chair

and sitting on my thumbs.
Soon it took all my resolve
to keep from shouting "Bravo"

after nearly every line;
five more minutes of this
and nothing would have stopped me

from rising, unbidden,
and burbling superlatives.
So I left.

As I tiptoed down the hall
I thought I heard the famous poet say:
"Now we can really begin."

II

Fire

The brain may be seen as hardware ... and the mind as software.
—British physiopsychologist Philip J. Corr

That's not all there is to it.

The fanatic mind is to the brain
what magma is to a volcano.

The depressed mind is to the brain
what guano is to the floor of a cave.

The paranoid mind is to the brain
what a soldier is to a foxhole.

The schizophrenic mind is to the brain
what a hyena is to a flimsy cage.

The narcissist's mind is to the brain
what a peacock's train is to the peacock.

The mind of a fool is to the brain
what a cow is to a piano.

The mind of a genius is to the brain
what galaxies are to the universe.

For others, at its best,
the mind is to the brain
what a fire is to a fireplace,

throwing off heat and light
on its way to the ash bin.

Heisenberg's Uncertainty Principle

Once, in college, I explained this
to a girl I was trying to impress.
Men are like that, she said,

you can't pin them down.
It was hopeless anyway. She tolerated me
only because she wanted my friend,

whose knowledge of physics was innate.
From across the table she gazed into my eyes,
took my hands and said,

tell me about Jim.
I told her the truth:
at a party he had dropped his pants,

lit a match,
and, for a moment,
transformed his ass into a jet engine.

She said she wished she had seen it.
I said I had lied.
She looked at me then with interest.

Subjunctive

The timid grammarian,
unable to approach the object
of his unspoken proposition,
is destined to dwell forever
alone in the woulds.

The Musician's Daughter

undresses for you,
murmuring,
My father beat my mother

and came to me,
and yes, he taught me
to play the flute,

so gently
you'll never be certain
my lips even touch it.

First Honeymoon
(Montreal, 1970)

In a gypsy café
three men toast us
with beer

and a chorus:
Deutschland, Deutschland
über alles,

über alles
in der Welt.
I raise my glass

like a shield
like a sword
and whisper to the fiddler

who smiles
and plays *Hava Negillah*
while I drink.

When my bride calls my behavior rude
I feel again
glass shattering under my foot.

Cruise Ship Intervention

God wakes from Her nap
in one of Her moods,

just in time to change the tide.
She puts on a rhinestone-studded jumpsuit,

purple stilettos and lipstick,
slings a boa around Her shoulders

and struts out on deck.
She's gorgeous, if you like that sort of thing.

And—admit it, pal—you do.
Yes, you, in the faded blue blazer,

staring over the railing,
working up the courage to jump.

I'd turn around if I were you.
Can't you feel the current shifting?

My Mother

chose not to return to the sea.
It had taken too long to get out,

a billion years, more or less,
wet-nursing trilobites,

dancing with sharks.
After a moment on the beach

she became a wisp of smoke
leaving traces of the ocean

in my daughter's eyes.

Tequila

After the storm
an upside-down sombrero floats by

with my head in it,
transformed into a lemon

with one slice missing.
I can't stop weeping,

yet even with the wound still fresh
I find solace in knowing

that the wayward wedge
has found romance

in the salty deep,
dancing with a consecrated worm.

The Poet Who Killed the Moon Pleads Guilty with an Explanation

When I was a boy
the moon was as real as my fist.
Later, like everyone else,
I tried to use it
to advance my career
and, when that failed,
to ignore it,
but it would not let me be.
Think of the torture I endured
staring up at the same tired simile
night after night,
praying for clouds.
Imagine the agony
of driving down a country road
lit by a stale metaphor,
or knowing that the tides
are ruled by a cliché.
I sought comfort in the things I could touch.
When the moon appeared in a cheese sandwich,
a tambourine,
a woman's face and buttocks,
I was driven to act.

But I think you will agree
I have suffered enough,
since every sentence I write
now ends with an eclipse.

III

Questions and Answers About Mustaches

1.

Is it true that there was once a constellation in the shape of a mustache?

Yes, but the ancients disallowed it.

2.

Why?

Because astrology is serious business.

3.

What makes a mustache funny?

A mustache resembles a bird in flight.
A man's upper lip does not resemble the sky.

4.

Should a woman choose a man with a mustache?

That depends
on whether she prefers to laugh with others
or giggle fitfully alone.

Valentine

What comes to mind
is that cheap hotel in Athens:
the sheets, flecked black
by countless washings
in oily water,
were nonetheless clean
and always extraordinary.

Twenty-two Years After Falling in Love with You

I ducked out of the snow
into a steamy bakery.

From behind a glass counter
the yeasty baker gazed at me

as though I could change the weather
or her life.

Then she prepared to speak.
Believe me love,

when I tell you
I lowered my eyes

and examined her strudel
as though it were sacred,

that part of you
I've not yet seen.

I sit astride life like a bad rider on a horse. I only owe it to the horse's good nature that I am not thrown off at this very moment.

—Ludwig Wittgenstein

Just Before Falling Asleep on a Bench near Wittgenstein's Grave

(Ascension Parish Burial Ground, Cambridge, England)

I notice a formidable black hen
pacing near the stone of the great philosopher,
who died on April 21, 1951,
having written, only hours before, while sedated,

Someone who, dreaming, says "I am dreaming,"
even if he speaks audibly while doing so,
is no more right than if he said in his dream
"it is raining," while it was in fact raining.
Even if his dream was connected with the noise of the rain.

Wittgenstein was wrong,
I tell the hen, who cocks her head.
Encouraged, I continue,
How does the fact that I am dreaming
invalidate the statement, "I am dreaming,"
or, for that matter, the statement,
"I am snoring," even if my dream
is graced by the rhythm of my snores?
But the chicken—who, I observe now,
is wearing a saddle and a bridle—mutters only,
I am dreaming.

Reluctant Return from England

I unpack slowly.
On deserted roads
I drive on the left.

In the evening I retreat to the garden,
where I read Shelley
by the light of Her Majesty's moon.

By day I hide among the leftovers
in my last piece of carry-on luggage:
a small umbrella,

a stale scone,
my travel alarm
set to tea time,

and the River Cam
on a postcard
addressed to my dead mother.

Journey to the Subconscious, Interrupted

You assemble your provisions:
rope, miner's headlamp,
canary in a cage,

the complete works of Kafka
and a secret map
sketched by a phrenologist.

You tie one end of the rope
to a steam pipe
in the basement of your childhood home,

toss the other into the abyss,
and are about to descend
when your mother appears

in her wedding dress:
I can't find your father.
You'll have to do the chores.

Degrees of Nudity
Paros, Greece, 1996

I.

At a beachfront hotel I meet
the strangers with whom I will study
modern Greek. The beach is sandy, sheltered,
clothing optional. There are degrees of nudity.
For women: bare-breasted,
and nude. For men:
nude, reclining;
nude playing volleyball;
and nude with cell phone,
small antenna gleaming.

II.

We students walk to the beach clothed, in clusters,
but one afternoon I go alone.
Two classmates, Marie and Souzana,
see me coming,
cover up quickly.
I ask, Why me? All these people …
Souzana says well, yes,
but *they* are strangers.
And I recall, just hours before,
the three of us
in a dark room,
conjugating.

Bricks

You're the one
with an affinity for bricks,
new ones piled on pallets,
still warm,
and the nicked and broken strays

that you bring home.
When we moved here,
you took up residence
beside the hearth,

where, on winter nights,
I find myself rising
like smoke,
or your sweet-smelling bread.

Rachel at Eight
(or, The News from Down Under)

I take her to the ocean at dusk,
watch her dive through the breakers

and emerge, laughing,
beneath a perfect half moon,

the other half down there
on the water,

dancing with her.
I figure the rest of my life

will be anticlimax
but the next day I hear her say,

Madeline, there are colors you and I
have never even heard of.

When Madeline asks where,
Rachel says Australia.

Time Travel in the Grand Canyon

My boy is too close to the edge,
scanning the cliffs for dinosaurs.

Maybe I should tell him how time accelerates,
how it took four billion years

for these rocks to form
but only thirty thousand

for the river to slice through them.
How last week,

when the wind blew a woman off the rim,
it took her less than a minute

to drop down through the ages,
her shadow on the canyon wall

already a ghost.

First Day of Swimming Therapy for a Boy Recovering from a Bone Infection While Reading The Diary of Anne Frank

Now, with his back to the pool,
he wobbles like a prisoner
on the edge of the grave

they've made him dig.
During those first days,
when fever and doctors overran him,

he took refuge in his wounded heel
and she joined him there,
deep in the bone,

where even X-rays could not find them.
When the pain got so bad
he confused it with sirens

she held his hand.
"When I'm sixteen," she said,
"you'll be thirteen,"

so he fought to reach thirteen.
Later he tried to escape
but his limp attracted attention.

He was captured,
interrogated,
brought here,

told to jump.
Now, in wonder,
he sees himself turn

and flutter down,
a leaf in an uncertain breeze.
He'll tell them nothing.

Snow

At the local diner I slip into a booth, which remains empty.

Cindy, a waitress, refills mugs from pots marked Good and Evil.

I take out a pen and write a letter of recommendation for a friend. It begins: "Dear God...."

Benny, the cook, emerges to bemoan the recent spike in platypus infestations.

A lion in the next booth leans over and says, "This seems okay until someone wanders in from the veldt, and then I remember how long it's been since I've gnawed on a zebra. Sometimes I even miss the vultures."

Outside, a small maple waves its branches wildly, like a cop shielding children from the sight of a corpse.

Snow melts like disappearing paper, leaving a ragged landscape of permanent ink.

My Next Poem

My next poem will be huge,
far too large for twelve-point type to hold.
It will shimmer across the sky like northern lights
and all who behold it will be changed.
My next poem will swallow black holes
as black holes swallow stars.
It will be bigger than the universe,
broader than time itself.
                        This poem, though,
concerns smaller things:
milk turning sour,
the spider in the bathtub,
the click at the other end of the line,
a hairline crack
in the ceiling over the bed.

IV

Keys

At 2 a.m.
in a strange part of town

I lock myself out of my car.
Through the window I can see

my keys in the ignition,
my mobile phone on the seat,

and, on the floor,
a note from a woman:

What has happened?
I feel a terrible distance between us.

A Message from Ugarte

You would find the conversation a trifle one-sided. Signor Ugarte is dead.
—Major Strasser to Victor Laszlo in *Casablanca*

Remember me? Wheedling, sycophantic, nasal, like a tissue on a comb.
You hated everything about me. You shivered with joy at my death.
Never mind. I'm the forgiving sort.
Come close. Let me tell you something. Life and death are not so different,

two sides of the same weighted coin. Signor Dante—did I tell you he's my friend?—
almost had it right. But there are hundreds of circles here,
and they're not so impermeable as he imagined. There is traffic among them—
unofficial, of course, and fraught with hazards. The traveler who sets off on his own

is bound to be waylaid by a false note, to wander vaguely into the maw of a peacock
he mistakes for paradise. But I can help.
You don't have to take my word for it. Ask Dante. We have served each other well.
In return for his trust, I arranged for him several covert views of Beatrice.

You believe me, don't you? But then you have no choice. When you arrive here,
blind and shoeless, you'll need a guide. For a reasonable price—
we'll worry about that later—I'll see that you get where you want to go.
Come. Where else can you find your letter of transit?

Appalachian Nocturne

Like Death, my father was a fatalist.
Some dogwoods never bloom,

he told me, trying to be kind.
When it came to music, though,

there was no similarity.
My father's piano brought Bach to life

while Death continues to murder him
with off-key bleats

on a cracked bone kazoo.
Usually near dawn,

as sleep and Father's grace
elude me again,

I am forced to remind myself
that blossoms aren't everything.

In Kentucky, for example, the early pioneers
scoured their teeth with dogwood bark.

The Request
(or, Etude in B Negative)

I approach a man, a woman and a Stradivarius cello on a snowy bench in Central Park.

The man has a goose on his lap. He plucks it like a lyre.

He apologizes for being Paderewski, whom he does not resemble.

The woman does resemble the cello.

She says she is glad to be here after so long in Shangri-La.

I slept with Bach, she assures me.

And I, says the Strad, have thrummed between the thighs of the greats.

I screw up my cornet and ask if I might sit in.

The goose says nothing.

Counter

Shortly after their twenty-third anniversary
They're on bar stools in an art deco lounge in Minneapolis,
knees touching. He's feeling lucky tonight, and why not?
He's been lucky, mostly, for twenty-three years.
She's staring down at the bar,
a worn slab of marble, white, black splotches, broad as a Holstein.
She drains her second martini, nods to herself, then tells him
she *knows* this stone:

Here, see the egg-shaped indentation near the edge?
Back in the '50's, this was the counter
in an ice cream parlor
in Portsmouth, New Hampshire,
where my father took me and my brother for banana splits

before his drinking got out of hand,
before he took to carrying a gun,
before our mother kicked him out.
Before she died.
Before my brother quit school
and bought that black cape.
Before drugs, the war,
my first husband.
Before the city tore the building down.
Before all that.

She moves her leg. The way she's rubbing the marble,
he knows better than to ask if she's sure.

coming out of a depression

sleet

gravel in a chicken's gut

flies buzzing feebly against a screen

crows

morels at the foot of a dead apple tree

shadow of a hawk, receding

whisper of snakes on stone

the sun that powers the heart of a flea

a history of oceans
written on the underside of clouds

in a worn wicker basket
abandoned by a stream,
galaxies blooming

Chickens

A man said to me,
Let's get these chickens registered.
There were no chickens.
The man had a tiny car.
We drove underneath the traffic,
looking for an airport.
The only place you can register a chicken is Missouri,
he explained. We couldn't find the airport
but he didn't mind.
The important thing, he said,
was to keep trying.

The Passion of the Eiffel Tower

Anne Carson, it is said,
prefers a one-line bio:
Anne Carson lives in Canada.

In a photo, her face
is sandstone,
hair chopped at the chin,

black-framed glasses
hollowed-out coins
unfit for Charon.

She avoids the camera
as though it were the sun.
On a website

her students at McGill
gave her a zero
in the Hotness Factor category.

And yet (*Fire. Time. Fire./
Choose, said God*), she burns.
She smolders (*from nipples to hard*)

like peat from her beloved moors,
or roars (*When I look at the city of Paris
I want to wrap my legs around it*)

like a furnace in the streets,
a conflagration in which I
glow red as an ingot.

Students are students for a reason,
after all,
and it was the cameraman,

not (*ravishing/in/her/armor*)
Anne, who turned away
to keep from melting.

How I Failed to Write This Poem
(and Why It's Not My Fault)

The poem appeared as a raincloud.
I undressed and flew through it.
The effect on the poem was unsettling:

it became, in rapid succession,
the Arctic ice cap,
the Sonora Desert in bloom,

the Great Barrier Reef,
and then, almost finally,
a snow-capped mountain

somewhere in the Andes.
I dressed and bought some crampons,
an ice axe, a rope

and a burro, and went to sleep.
During the night
the burro chewed through the rope

and the poem became a storm-swept ocean
south of the equator.
In the time it took me to rent a boat,

arrange for scuba lessons
and stock up on shark repellant,
the tide went out.

It never came back.
I blame the moon,
which was not supposed to be in this poem at all.

V

Diner, Revere, Massachusetts, Winter, 4 a.m.

Coffee? You look tired, hon.

She brings the coffee. It's just the two of us, the waitress's grey braid down to her ass, my stubble vibrant. Pretend it's summer, she says. Illusion helps. You know the drill: an asphalt road is a river of magma. Windswept snow is a witch's veil. How do you want your eggs?

Laid by Druid chickens, I say, playing along. Sunny side down.

How old are you?

Sixty-one in human years. An artist friend says my life is a cubist self-portrait, subtly layered—infinite eyebrows, she says, a girl could lose herself in those. If you ask me, I'm a bottle of bad scotch, three-quarters gone.

The waitress sits down, pours herself some coffee. Your artist, is she genuine? Does she swim naked in the North Atlantic? Has she an affinity for men in lace? Is she drawn to tequila and other wormy things? Can she spin shit into steel?

She pats my hand. It's all right, hon, she says. There's no such thing as bad scotch.

The Way Women Are

She says there's no reason for me to be jealous,
even though he's good with his hands,
which I'm not. They've been friends
for longer than she's known me,
but that's all, she says.
He's aged gracefully, hair still black
as the mustache on his lean face.

Last night he came over for dinner.
We drank some whiskey. He talked about being old.
I'm working part-time, he said.
I'm interested in taking a nap, and reading,
and taking another nap.
It's different now. I'm in the last quarter.
Maybe the last third, I said. I'm older than he is.

We drank more whiskey. After a while
she said he'd better sleep on the couch.
Later she kissed me. As usual,
she said I had nothing to worry about.
As usual, there was no sign she was lying.
So skillful—
the way women are about these things.

Bodyguard

He was a big fellow, broad-shouldered.

His wife was tiny and lame.

He swaggered through London.

She limped along behind him,
swatting at pickpockets with her crutch.

One of the Starving Children in Europe Absolves Me

In Athens, says Dimitra,
first the Nazis,
then the civil war—

we ate cockroaches, rats,
nothing. My little sister was five
when she cracked a tooth

on an old pigeon wing,
closed her eyes, nodded,
and died.

You, in New York,
not eating your broccoli—
you had nothing to do with it.

I'm the one
who picked up that bone
and kept on gnawing.

Advice My Daughter Will Probably Ignore

When some guy floats up out of nowhere
and says he's a poet and a writer
who drinks more than is good for him,
plus he doesn't care,
and his friends are all fucked up
or dead,
and the guy pulls out his wallet
and shows you hundred-dollar bills
and tells you—
only you, he says—
he wants to walk with you by the railroad track
because you're the only one who can teach him—
if anybody can teach him it's you, he says,
because you've got eyes and thighs that remind him
of somebody, years ago, probably dead now,
who had eyes and thighs a lot like yours,
and he's been sleeping on the couch ever since,
but if he can only lick this barrage of fucking
words that keep coming,
no matter what he does—
if you can teach him, you know, to be, at least a little
concise, well then,
he'll take you out on his boat
and you'll have a terrific time
no matter *what*—
storms, sharks, lousy music, whatever—
if he says those things,
you have a right to be suspicious,
because, well,
by then,
you'll have heard it all before.

At 65

When you were ten it seemed as old as China,
and as distant.

Now one of your goals appears within reach:
death in old age. When it comes it will feel

like the quiet of an empty house.
Meanwhile, you find yourself astonished

by the texture of clouds,
the taste of table wine,

the gentle ache in your left knee,
your wife at the piano, playing Bach.

Immortality in a Minor Key

I'm a spruce tree.
All right, I'm not a spruce tree.
It's been a rough week.
Next best thing,

I'm out here in the woods,
talking with spruce trees.
The conversation is desultory.
A few of my companions

dream of leaving the forest.
Not a good plan, I tell them.
Look at you, all bent and knotty.
Not for you the captain's chair,

the widow's walk.
Why, you're not even fit
for the false floor of the gallows.
You'll wind up as cardboard

or firewood, or worse:
sawdust on a cow barn floor.
Besides, I say,
you can take the tree out of the forest,

but you can't take the forest out of the tree.
Take my word for it, you're better off here.
To prove it I take root,
but it's a shallow gesture.

I know I can't stay
when every fiber of my being
yearns to shelter
the soul of a cello.

Finding the Potato

*Inside of one potato
there are mountains and rivers.*
    —Shinkichi Takahashi (trans. Harold Wright)

But how to find that one potato
among all the others?
Patience, my friend.
Put your ear to the ground.
Dig where you hear thunder.

VI

Late Harvest

There's no shame in it, old man:
from the compost of your mind

a young girl sprouts,
buds and ripens,

smelling of earth and dew.
Vines encircle your ancient trunk.

Your mouth drops open.
The fruit—you shiver.

Never have you tasted
anything this sweet.

Outside, snow piling up fast.

Floater

It happens as you get older—
something breaks loose from a retina.

Close your eyes,
turn your face toward the light

and there it is,
a dark speck

swirling through your field of vision,
an amoeba on a slide,

a plane flying loop-the-loops,
a dancer

enjoying her last moments
on the stage.

Last Peach

Lopsided, speckled, pale,
picked hard ahead of the frost.

Let it lie for three days,

then taste the remains of summer,
five tart bites.

A Widow at 93

She says she's surviving,
by which she means she's dying

slowly. As a precaution,
every night she tells her pillow

goodbye. *Survive* is a sharp word;
the v's cut like shivs.

A ruthless verb,
indifferent to the objects

it has taken:
father, mother,

husband, brother,
son

The Death of a Scholar

He watches himself bleed out in the rain,
his left leg, in denim, not far off.
The Harley he loved like a lover

lies with its back to him,
twisted and smoking.
He tries to think of his wife,

but instead, feeling himself disappear,
he remembers the story
of General Antonio López de Santa Anna,

who arranged for the interment
of his own amputated leg
in a national shrine,

and of the ungrateful peasants
who, when the general was deposed,
dragged it through the streets.

Advice to a Weary Traveler

Allow yourself to be enticed
by a whiff of sulfur.

Slip through a fissure
in the cliff face

of a volcanic island
in the Aegean.

Now ease your way down
a rough stone tunnel,

hundreds of feet
to a small cave,

once the hiding place
of fugitives.

Here the air is warm and dry
as the hearth in the kitchen

of your childhood home.
Kneel. You'll find initials

scratched in the floor
near a piece of bone,

the top half of someone's skull.
Pick it up.

See how neatly it fits in your hand,
like a shell

or the smooth wooden bowl
from which you served olives

long ago,
when you lived on the surface.

Alchemy

A year after his death,
following instructions,
she pours herself a glass of wine

and opens his letter:
If it pleases you, love,
write a book about us.

Make something gorgeous
out of everything, even
the maggots in the cellar,

the mold in the pantry,
the tarantula perched on the bedpost.
Go deep, as they say

in football, geology,
philosophy, sex.
Don't forget:

in the Dark Ages
the main ingredient
of the ink used by monks

to illuminate their texts,
one glorious letter at a time,
was urine.

Your Date with Death

starts with low expectations.
You don't even bother to shave.
Well, forget what you've heard about her.

She's Wendy, your high school sweetheart,
still eighteen, dressed in white.
(How could you have dumped her?)

She takes your hand
and you think peaches, waterfalls,
the smell of suntan lotion

on bare shoulders.
Now you can finally dance—
not the tango you once craved,

but a mannered waltz
in a mirrored ballroom,
ending with a curtsy and a bow.

Later, at her door, she thanks you.
Feeling shy, you ask,
What's it like, being Death?

On good nights, she says,
it's like this,
and she kisses you hard.

Judgment Day

A pig slits my throat.

A fish disembowels me.

A lobster drops me in boiling water.

An ant the size of a building steps on me.

A spider inadvertently tosses me into a fire
along with the wood.

A frog puts me in a jar filled with chloroform
and screws on the lid.

But also,
a turtle I've removed from the path of a car
takes me aside
and explains.

Acknowledgments

"Rachel at Eight" and "My Mother," *Conscience*, Spring, 2001

"Chickens" and "Immortality in a Minor Key," *Cranky Literary Journal*, May, 2005

"Floater," *Alaska Quarterly Review*, Fall & Winter, 2005

"Advice to a Weary Traveler," *The Powhatan Review*, Winter, 2005

"First Day of Swimming Therapy for a Boy Recovering from a Bone Infection While Reading *The Diary of Anne Frank*," *Paper Street*, Spring, 2006

"Shrimp," *Cranky Literary Journal* May, 2006

"Degrees of Nudity," *The Powhatan Review*, Summer, 2006

"A Widow at 93," *The Bellevue Literary Review*, Fall, 2006

"Late Harvest," *Arch and Quiver*, Fall, 2006

"Soap," *Comstock Review*, Fall/Winter, 2006

"Bipolar," *The American Journal of Nursing*, May, 2007

"Diner, Revere, Massachusetts, Winter, 4 a.m." and "Time Travel in The Grand Canyon," *Silk Road*, Spring, 2008

"Snow," *Tuesday; An Art Project*, Spring, 2010

"The Death of a Scholar" and "Your Date with Death," *Alaska Quarterly Review*, Spring and Summer, 2010

"Alchemy," "Fire" and "Judgment Day," *Jerseyworks*, Spring, 2011

"Evidence that We Are Descended from Chairs," *Comstock Review*, Spring/Summer 2011

"Finding the Potato," "Keys" and "Subjunctive," *Bigger Than They Appear: Anthology of Very Short Poems*, Accents Publishing, 2011

"Cruise Ship Intervention," *Third Wednesday*, Winter, 2011

"Reluctant Return from England," *Comstock Review*, Fall/Winter 2011/2012

About the Author

Andrew Merton has been a political reporter and columnist for the *Gloucester* (Massachusetts) *Times, The Boston Herald Traveler* and the *Boston Globe,* and a contributing editor with *Boston Magazine.* His articles and essays have also appeared in *The New York Times Magazine, Esquire, Ms. Magazine, Yankee Magazine* and *The Boston Phoenix.* His book *Enemies of Choice* was published by Beacon Press in 1980, and his anthology *In Your Own Voice: A Writer's Reader* was published by HarperCollins in 1995. His poetry has appeared in *The Alaska Quarterly Review, Bellevue Literary Review, Powhatan Review, Paper Street, The Comstock Review, Silk Road, Third Wednesday, The American Journal of Nursing* and elsewhere. He teaches writing at the University of New Hampshire.

Chapbooks by Accents Publishing

The Deer at Gethsemani: Eclogues by Frederick Smock
Fading Into Bolivia by Richard Taylor
Animal Time by Greg Pape
Ants by Denyo Denev
How Swallowtails Become Dragons by Bianca Spriggs
Numbered Bones by Bobby Steve Baker
Of a Bed Frame by Dan Nowak
Bloom on a Split Board by Nana Lampton
Original Ruse by Barbara Sabol
Bee-coursing Box by Matthew Haughton
Metes and Bounds by J. Kates
Plein Jeu by E. C. Belli
Meeting Dad by Brian Russell
Wrecking Ball and Other Urban Haiku by Barry George
The View from Down Here by Jude Lally
Stick Tight Man by Jim Lally

Full-Length World Poetry Series by Accents Publishing

No. 1   *Etcetera's Mistress* by Thom Ward

www.ingramcontent.com/pod-product-compliance
Lightning Source LLC
Chambersburg PA
CBHW021156080526
44588CB00008B/367